CELEBRATING THE NAME AUSTIN

Celebrating the Name Austin

Walter the Educator

Silent King Books

SILENT KING BOOKS

SKB

Copyright © 2024 by Walter the Educator

All rights reserved. No part of this book may be reproduced in any manner whatsoever without written permission except in the case of brief quotations embodied in critical articles and reviews.

First Printing, 2024

Disclaimer
This book is a literary work; poems are not about specific persons, locations, situations, and/or circumstances unless mentioned in a historical context. This book is for entertainment and informational purposes only. The author and publisher offer this information without warranties expressed or implied. No matter the grounds, neither the author nor the publisher will be accountable for any losses, injuries, or other damages caused by the reader's use of this book. The use of this book acknowledges an understanding and acceptance of this disclaimer.

dedicated to everyone with the first name of Austin

AUSTIN

In dawn's gentle embrace, where sunlight gleams,

AUSTIN

Awakens Austin, bearer of dreams,

AUSTIN

A name that whispers through ancient trees,

AUSTIN

A tale of wonder carried by the breeze.

AUSTIN

A is for ambition, a beacon so bright,

AUSTIN

Guiding through darkness, a radiant light.

AUSTIN

Uplifted by courage, steadfast and true,

AUSTIN

Austin, your spirit, the world does renew.

AUSTIN

Sunrise in the heart, a golden flare,

AUSTIN

Turning night's shadows into morning's care.

AUSTIN

In every breath, a melody sings,

AUSTIN

Navigating life on resilient wings.

AUSTIN

Tender are the moments where you tread,

AUSTIN

Bringing forth visions where others dread.

AUSTIN

Your name, Austin, carved in history's scroll,

AUSTIN

A journey of wisdom, a seeker's role.

AUSTIN

Upon the hills where eagles soar high,

AUSTIN

Austin's resolve touches the sky.

AUSTIN

Nurturing dreams with a fervent embrace,

AUSTIN

Each step you take, a destined grace.

AUSTIN

With eyes like the ocean, deep and serene,

AUSTIN

A mind ever curious, thoughts pristine.

AUSTIN

Austin, the seeker, of truths yet found,

AUSTIN

In every whisper, in every sound.

AUSTIN

Beneath the stars, a celestial dance,

AUSTIN

Where fate and fortune find their chance.

AUSTIN

In Austin's name, a legacy grand,

AUSTIN

A touch of magic in a mortal's hand.

AUSTIN

Voices of the past in chorus sing,

AUSTIN

Austin, the harbinger of spring.

AUSTIN

Echoes of courage, of battles won,

AUSTIN

In your essence, a thousand suns.

AUSTIN

Paths untrodden, where few dare to stride,

AUSTIN

Austin ventures with honor as guide.

AUSTIN

In every heartbeat, a drum of might,

AUSTIN

Leading the way from darkness to light.

AUSTIN

In dreams fulfilled, in quests pursued,

AUSTIN

Austin, the essence of fortitude.

AUSTIN

ABOUT THE CREATOR

Walter the Educator is one of the pseudonyms for Walter Anderson. Formally educated in Chemistry, Business, and Education, he is an educator, an author, a diverse entrepreneur, and he is the son of a disabled war veteran. "Walter the Educator" shares his time between educating and creating. He holds interests and owns several creative projects that entertain, enlighten, enhance, and educate, hoping to inspire and motivate you.

Follow, find new works, and stay up to date
with Walter the Educator™
at WaltertheEducator.com

www.ingramcontent.com/pod-product-compliance
Lightning Source LLC
LaVergne TN
LVHW051921060526
838201LV00060B/4123